THIS BOOK BELONGS TO...

Name: Age:

Favourite player:

2018/2019

My Predictions...	Actual...
The Foxes' final position:	
The Foxes' top scorer:	
Premier League Winners:	
Premier League top scorer:	
FA Cup Winners:	
EFL Cup Winners:	

Contributors: Peter Rogers

A TWOCAN PUBLICATION

ISBN 978-1-912692-29-3

CONTENTS

01 KASPER **SCHMEICHEL**

GOALKEEPER   DOB: 05/11/86   COUNTRY: DENMARK

One of the Premier League's most talented goalkeepers and part of the Foxes' 2015/16 title-winning team, Schmeichel joined Leicester from Leeds United in 2011. After starring for Denmark in the 2018 World Cup finals in Russia, he agreed a new deal with the Foxes in August 2018.

SQUAD 2018/19

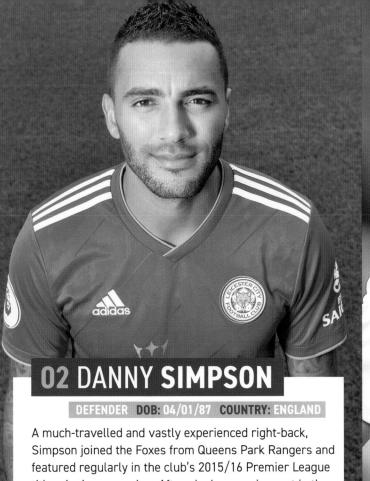

02 DANNY **SIMPSON**

DEFENDER   DOB: 04/01/87   COUNTRY: ENGLAND

A much-travelled and vastly experienced right-back, Simpson joined the Foxes from Queens Park Rangers and featured regularly in the club's 2015/16 Premier League title-winning campaign. After playing a major part in the Premier League success he then represented the club in the 2016-17 UEFA Champions League campaign.

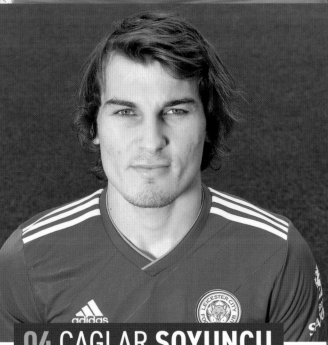

04 CAGLAR **SOYUNCU**

DEFENDER   DOB: 23/05/96   COUNTRY: TURKEY

Young Turkish defender Soyuncu joined the Foxes on deadline day during the summer 2018 transfer window. A tall and particularly mobile defender, he was signed from Bundesliga side SC Freiburg. Although currently aged just 22 he has already won over a dozen caps for the Turkish national side.

03 BEN **CHILWELL**

DEFENDER   DOB: 21/12/96   COUNTRY: ENGLAND

A product of the Foxes' Academy set-up, Chilwell has progressed through the ranks to make the left-back berth his own. A player with bags of potential, he loves to break forward and support attacking moves whenever possible. His form at club level has been rewarded with a number of call-ups to the England under-21 squad and after a superb start to the 2018/19 season, he was called up to the England squad by Gareth Southgate, making his senior debut in a 1-0 win over Switzerland at King Power Stadium.

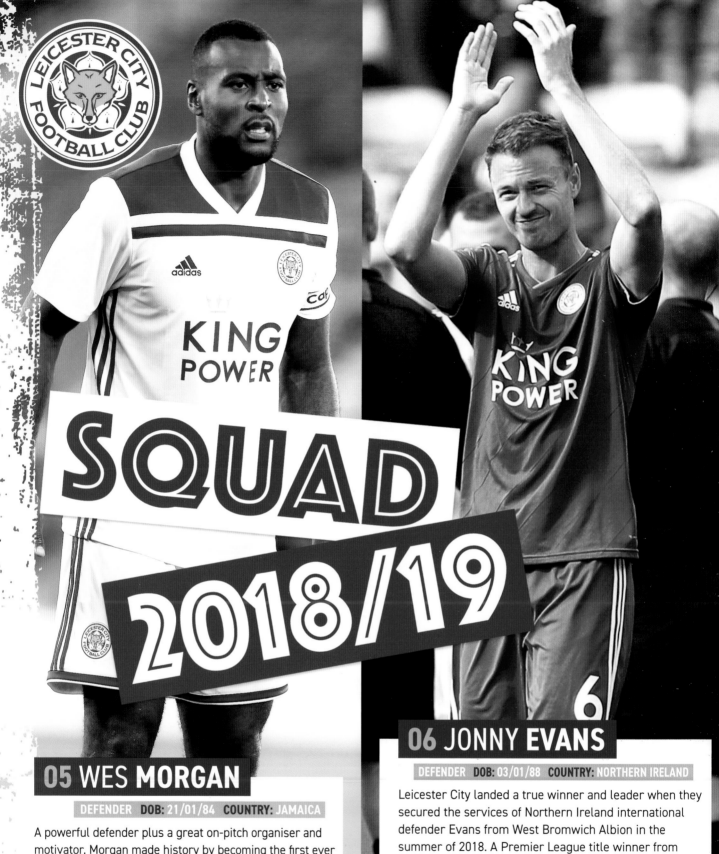

SQUAD 2018/19

05 WES MORGAN

DEFENDER   DOB: 21/01/84   **COUNTRY:** JAMAICA

A powerful defender plus a great on-pitch organiser and motivator, Morgan made history by becoming the first ever Leicester City player to lift the Premier League trophy after captaining the side to the title in 2016. Morgan was ever-present in the title-winning season and his contribution was rewarded in July 2016 with a new three-year deal that ties him to the King Power until 2019.

06 JONNY EVANS

DEFENDER   DOB: 03/01/88   **COUNTRY:** NORTHERN IRELAND

Leicester City landed a true winner and leader when they secured the services of Northern Ireland international defender Evans from West Bromwich Albion in the summer of 2018. A Premier League title winner from his time at Manchester United, Evans has also won over 70 caps for Northern Ireland.

07 DEMARAI **GRAY**

MIDFIELDER **DOB:** 28/06/96 **COUNTRY:** ENGLAND

Widely looked upon as one of the brightest talents in English football, Gray joined the Foxes from Birmingham City in January 2016. A speedy winger who can operate down either flank, he possesses wonderful close control and has an eye for goal too. Already a Premier League champion and England under-21 international.

08 KELECHI **IHEANACHO**

STRIKER **DOB:** 03/10/96 **COUNTRY:** NIGERIA

Lively frontman Iheanacho joined the Foxes from Premier League rivals Manchester City in August 2017. His arrival at the King Power saw him link up with fellow Nigeria internationals Wilfred Ndidi and Ahmed Musa among the Leicester ranks. He netted eight goals in his first season with the club and also featured for Nigeria in the World Cup finals in the summer.

09 JAMIE **VARDY**

STRIKER **DOB:** 11/01/87 **COUNTRY:** ENGLAND

The star man at the King Power Stadium and hero of the club's Premier League success in 2015/16, Vardy loves to chase and hassle defenders. A clinical finisher, he remains the focal point of the Leicester attack and netted the club's first goal of the 2018/19 campaign in a narrow 2-1 defeat to Manchester United in the opening game of the season.

10 JAMES **MADDISON**

MIDFIELDER DOB: 23/11/96 COUNTRY: ENGLAND

Signed from Norwich City in the summer, Maddison is a highly-rated midfield playmaker. His performances at Carrow Road saw him voted the Canaries' Player of the Season in 2017/18 and he has already produced a number of eye-catching displays in a Foxes' shirt. This England under-21 star is certainly one to watch.

SQUAD 2018/19

11 MARC **ALBRIGHTON**

MIDFIELDER **DOB:** 18/11/89 **COUNTRY:** ENGLAND

Winger Albrighton was signed from Midlands rivals Aston Villa in May 2014 following the Foxes' return to the top flight. His ability to glide past full-backs and deliver accurate balls into the danger area has become a regular sight at the King Power Stadium. He now boasts over 150 appearances for Leicester and a goal tally that sits in double figures.

12 DANNY **WARD**

GOALKEEPER **DOB:** 22/06/93 **COUNTRY:** WALES

A full Wales international, goalkeeper Ward joined the Foxes from Liverpool on a four-year deal in July 2018. He produced a string of impressive performances to help Huddersfield to Premier League promotion via the play-offs in 2016/17 while on loan with the Terriers. His arrival at the King Power provides both competition and cover for Kasper Schmeichel.

14 RICARDO **PEREIRA**

DEFENDER **DOB:** 06/10/93 **COUNTRY:** PORTGUAL

Ricardo signed a five-year deal with Leicester City in June 2018, after five years with FC Porto. The speedy right-back, who can also operate as a winger, made 43 appearances for Porto in all competitions in 2017/18, and helped the side to the Portuguese league title. A full Portugal international, he made his Foxes' debut in the opening Premier League game of the season.

15 HARRY **MAGUIRE**

DEFENDER **DOB:** 05/03/93 **COUNTRY:** ENGLAND

An outstanding central defender, Maguire enjoyed a memorable first season with the Foxes after joining from Hull City in the summer of 2017. His performances at the heart of the defence saw him voted the club's Player of the Season and he ended a fantastic debut campaign with a host of impressive performances for England at the World Cup finals as the Three Lions reached the semi-finals.

SQUAD
2018/19

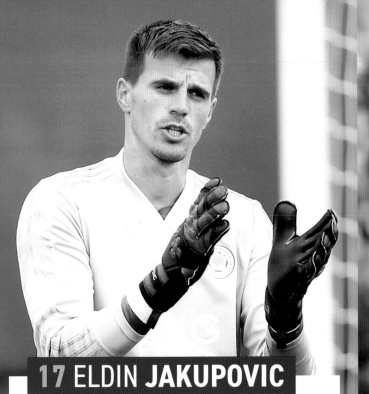

17 ELDIN **JAKUPOVIC**

GOALKEEPER DOB: 02/10/84 **COUNTRY:** SWITZERLAND

An experienced goalkeeper with assured handling skills and great shot stopping ability, Swiss stopper Jakupovic joined the Foxes from Hull City in the July 2017. He made his Leicester City debut in the FA Cup, playing in both the initial tie and replay against Fleetwood in January 2018 - keeping a clean sheet on both occasions.

18 DANIEL **AMARTEY**

MIDFIELDER DOB: 21/12/94 **COUNTRY:** GHANA

Ghanaian international Amartey joined the Foxes in January 2016 during the club's Premier League title-winning campaign. After signing from Copenhagen, Amartey made his debut in a vital 1-0 win over Norwich City in February 2016. A powerful ball-winning presence in the Foxes' midfield, he can also operate in defence if needed.

20 SHINJI **OKAZAKI**

STRIKER DOB: 16/04/86 **COUNTRY:** JAPAN

A proven goalscorer for both club and country, Okazaki joined the Foxes from FSV Mainz 05 in 2015 and has become a real fans' favourite at the King Power. An all-action frontman who never stops running, he has great strength on the ball and remains cool in one-on-one situations. He scored seven goals for the club last season and was another Leicester player to represent his country at the 2018 World Cup finals.

SQUAD 2018/19

22 MATTY JAMES

MIDFIELDER **DOB: 22/07/91** **COUNTRY: ENGLAND**

James signed for the Foxes back in 2012, when the club made a double swoop on Manchester United for James and teammate Richie De Laet. An athletic midfielder and real box-to-box player, he made his Leicester City debut together with Jamie Vardy in a 4-0 League Cup victory over Torquay United in August 2012. He made 15 first team appearances in all competitions last season.

21 VICENTE IBORRA

MIDFIELDER **DOB: 16/01/88** **COUNTRY: SPAIN**

Tenacious midfield dynamo Iborra provides an impressive work-rate in the heart of the Foxes' engine room. The experienced Spaniard completed his dream move to the Premier League when he joined Leicester from Sevilla in July 2017. After scoring three goals from midfield last season, he notched his first of 2018/19 in the 4-0 League Cup victory over Fleetwood.

23 ADRIEN SILVA

MIDFIELDER **DOB: 15/03/89** **COUNTRY: PORTUGAL**

A European Championship winner with Portugal in 2016, Silva brings a real touch of class and guile to the Foxes' midfield. Known for his dribbling and passing skills, he joined the Foxes in the summer of 2017. He featured in a dozen Premier League fixtures last season and also represented his country in the 2018 World Cup finals.

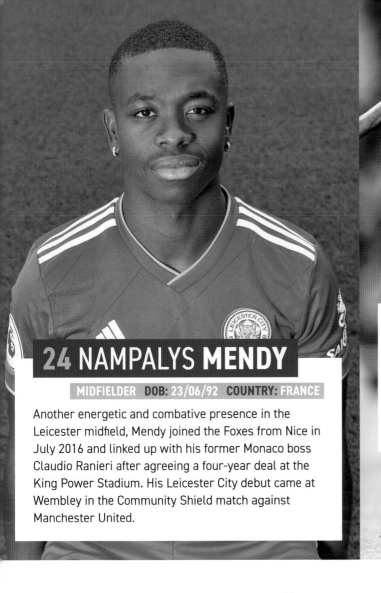

24 NAMPALYS **MENDY**

MIDFIELDER DOB: 23/06/92 COUNTRY: FRANCE

Another energetic and combative presence in the Leicester midfield, Mendy joined the Foxes from Nice in July 2016 and linked up with his former Monaco boss Claudio Ranieri after agreeing a four-year deal at the King Power Stadium. His Leicester City debut came at Wembley in the Community Shield match against Manchester United.

25 WILFRED **NDIDI**

MIDFIELDER DOB: 16/12/96 COUNTRY: NIGERIA

One of the first names on the Leicester City teamsheet, midfielder Ndidi made 38 appearances in all competitions for the Foxes in 2017/18. The Nigerian joined the club from Belgian side Genk in the 2017 January transfer window and has become a crowd favourite at the King Power.

27 FOUSSENI **DIABATE**

STRIKER DOB: 18/10/95 COUNTRY: MALI

A January 2018 acquisition from Gazelec Ajaccio, Mali youth international Diabate marked his Foxes' debut with two goals in a comprehensive 5-1 FA Cup victory away to Peterborough United. He made a total of 16 appearances in all competitions last season and was back in the first team fold for this season's League Cup victory over Fleetwood in August.

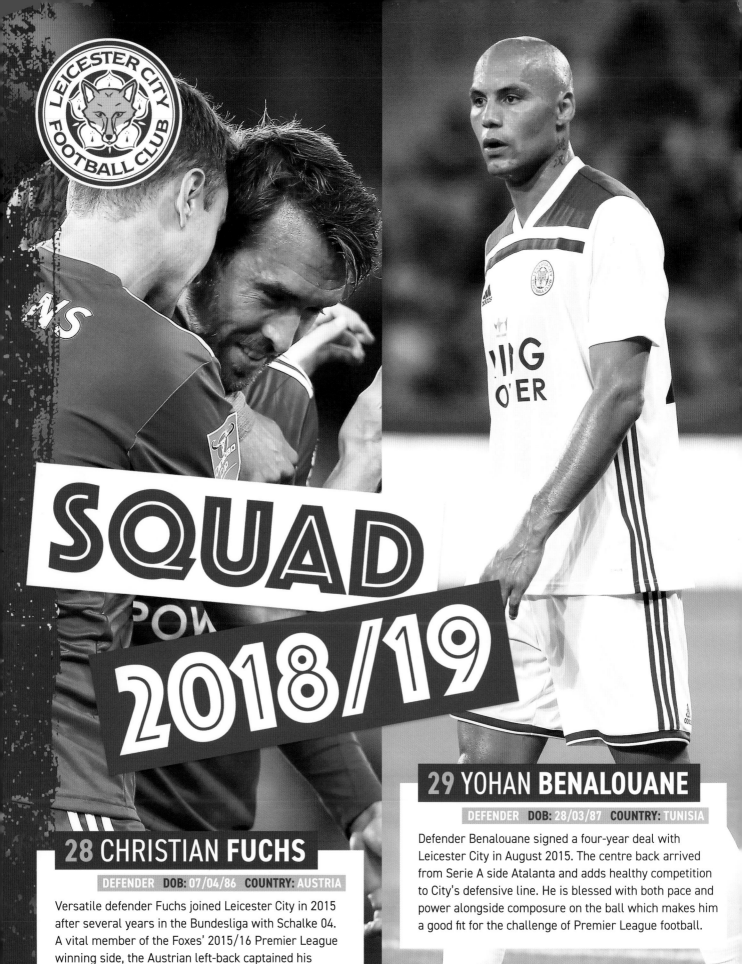

SQUAD 2018/19

29 YOHAN **BENALOUANE**

DEFENDER **DOB:** 28/03/87 **COUNTRY:** TUNISIA

Defender Benalouane signed a four-year deal with Leicester City in August 2015. The centre back arrived from Serie A side Atalanta and adds healthy competition to City's defensive line. He is blessed with both pace and power alongside composure on the ball which makes him a good fit for the challenge of Premier League football.

28 CHRISTIAN **FUCHS**

DEFENDER **DOB:** 07/04/86 **COUNTRY:** AUSTRIA

Versatile defender Fuchs joined Leicester City in 2015 after several years in the Bundesliga with Schalke 04. A vital member of the Foxes' 2015/16 Premier League winning side, the Austrian left-back captained his country at Euro 2016 before announcing his retirement from international football soon after.

31 RACHID **GHEZZAL**

MIDFIELDER **DOB:** 09/05/92 **COUNTRY:** ALGERIA

After joining the Foxes in August 2018 from Monaco, Algerian international winger Ghezzal made a flying start to his Leicester City career. The 26-year-old netted twice in his first four outings for the club to swiftly impress the King Power faithful. Ghezzal certainly looks set to thrill the fans on a regular basis over the months ahead.

38 HAMZAH **CHOUDHURY**

MIDFIELDER **DOB:** 01/10/97 **COUNTRY:** ENGLAND

Another exciting prospect to progress from the club's Academy, Choudhury is a tough-tackling talent in the centre of midfield who acts as a defensive guard in front of the back line. The youngster has benefited from his experience gained while on loan at Burton Albion and now appears set to develop his career further at the King Power.

37 ANDY **KING**

MIDFIELDER **DOB:** 29/10/88 **COUNTRY:** WALES

Wales international midfielder King is very much 'Mr Leicester City' among the current squad. He progressed through the club's Academy and made his first team debut in 2007. King has gone on to play over 375 times for Leicester City and has helped the club win the League One title, the Championship and the Premier League. A true Foxes' legend!

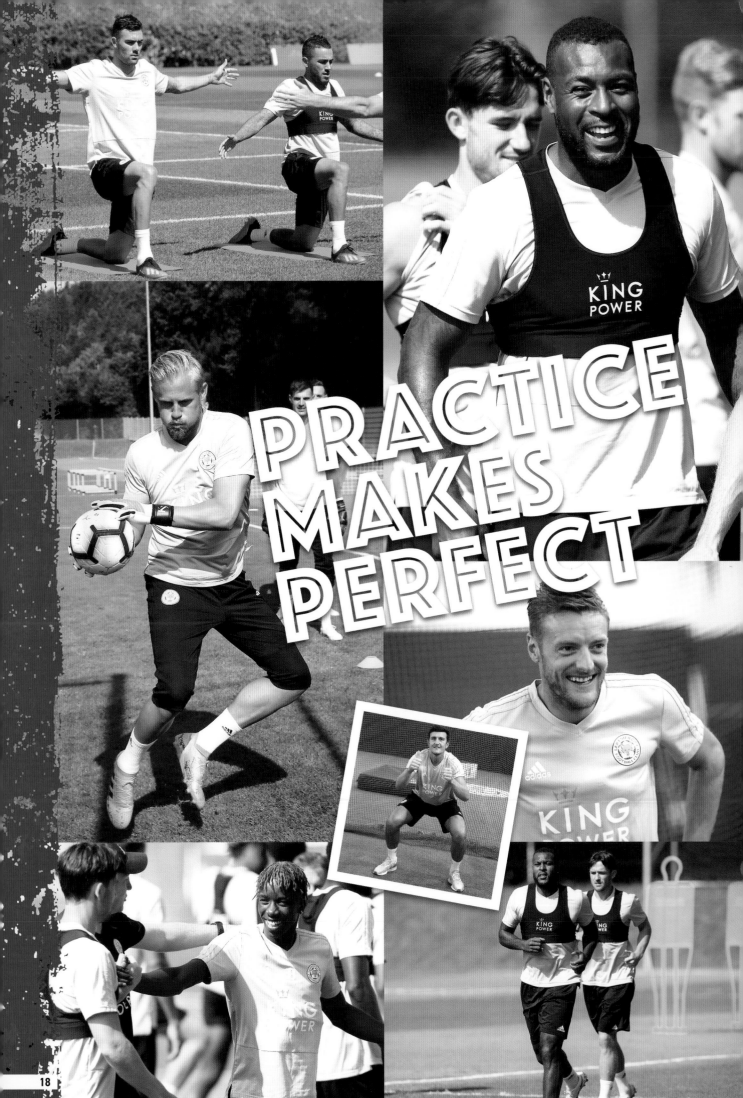

PRACTICE MAKES PERFECT

Practice, preparation and perseverance are all well-known key ingredients to success in the modern game. Long before the Foxes run out at King Power Stadium, they will have gone through a thorough and detailed spell of work at the club's busy training centre.

The Foxes' training ground is geared up to ensure that Claude Puel's men are fully equipped for the Premier League challenges that lie ahead. The modern-day player will not only be given the best of surfaces to practice on, but also given the very best advice and guidance in terms of their fitness, diet, rest and mental approach to performing at their maximum.

A typical day will begin with a series of physical tests, being weighed and taking part in a number of aerobic exercises, before blood levels and heart rates are measured.

Diet is vital to any player's wellbeing and performance levels, so a suitable breakfast is provided before the players head to the gymnasium to enjoy their own personal work-outs.

Prior to taking to the training pitches, players will be provided with a GPS tracking system and heart rate analysis monitors ensuring that all they do can be measured, monitored and reviewed. Then the physical conditioning begins out on the pitches. The manager and coaches will get down to working on various drills, set-piece situations and practice matches in the day's main session.

After a warm-down programme, it's off for a healthy lunch and a return to the gym for a strength, power and injury presentation session and feedback on the day's activities will be provided to the manager, coaches and players by the sports science department.

Come match day, this is where all the team's hard work and dedication through the week will make the difference.

KASPER
SCHMEICHEL

BORN:

18 SEPTEMBER 1949 · LEICESTER

POSITION:

GOALKEEPER

FOXES DEBUT:

LEICESTER CITY 3-0 EVERTON
DIVISION ONE · 4 MAY 1966

ALL CLUBS:

LEICESTER CITY, STOKE CITY, NOTTINGHAM FOREST, SOUTHAMPTON,
DERBY COUNTY, PLYMOUTH ARGYLE, BOLTON WANDERERS, LEYTON ORIENT

FOXES APPEARANCES:

APPEARANCES	LEAGUE	FA CUP	LEAGUE CUP	OTHERS
348	286	33	20	9

FOXES GOALS:

GOALS	LEAGUE
1	1

STAT ATTACK
PETER SHILTON

Goalkeeper Peter Shilton began training
with the Foxes as a 13-year-old. He soon impressed
all at Filbert Street and such was his potential he was
handed a first team debut in May 1966 aged just 16.

His breakthrough season came in 1967/68 after Gordon Banks had joined Stoke City. The following campaign
was one of mixed fortunes for the Foxes who suffered relegation from the First Division but reached the FA
Cup final where Shilton became one of the youngest ever goalkeepers to appear in the Wembley showpiece.

Leicester spent the following two seasons in the Second Division but Shilton's form was such that he was
handed his England debut against East Germany in November 1970 and a little over six months later
he was celebrating club success as the Foxes won the Second Division title.

In November 1974 Shilton followed in Banks' footsteps when he left the Foxes to join high-flying Stoke City.

ENGLAND INTERNATIONAL:

APPEARANCES
125

INTERNATIONAL DEBUT:

25 NOVEMBER 1970 - ENGLAND 3-1 EAST GERMANY

SPOT THE DIFFERENCE

Can you find the eight differences between these celebration photos?

KELECHI IHEANACHO

Magic MOMENT 120'

GOING Up

LEICESTER CITY FOOTBALL CLUB

FIXTURE: Endsleigh League Division One Play-Off final

DATE: Monday, 27 May 1996

SCORE: Leicester City 2 Crystal Palace 1

VENUE: Wembley

ATTENDANCE: 73,573

Steve Claridge was the Foxes' Wembley hero when his last-gasp extra-time winner secured victory in 1996 First Division Play-Off final.

Leicester had landed sixth place in the league and had overcome Stoke City in the semi-final to tee-up this Wembley date with Crystal Palace.

Hot favourites Palace took the lead through midfielder Andy Roberts after 14 minutes, and all looked to be going the Eagles' way until Garry Parker netted an equaliser from the penalty spot 14 minutes from time.

The match went into extra-time and then amazingly with penalties just two seconds away, Claridge struck the winner from the edge of the area to send the travelling Leicester fans into utter delirium.

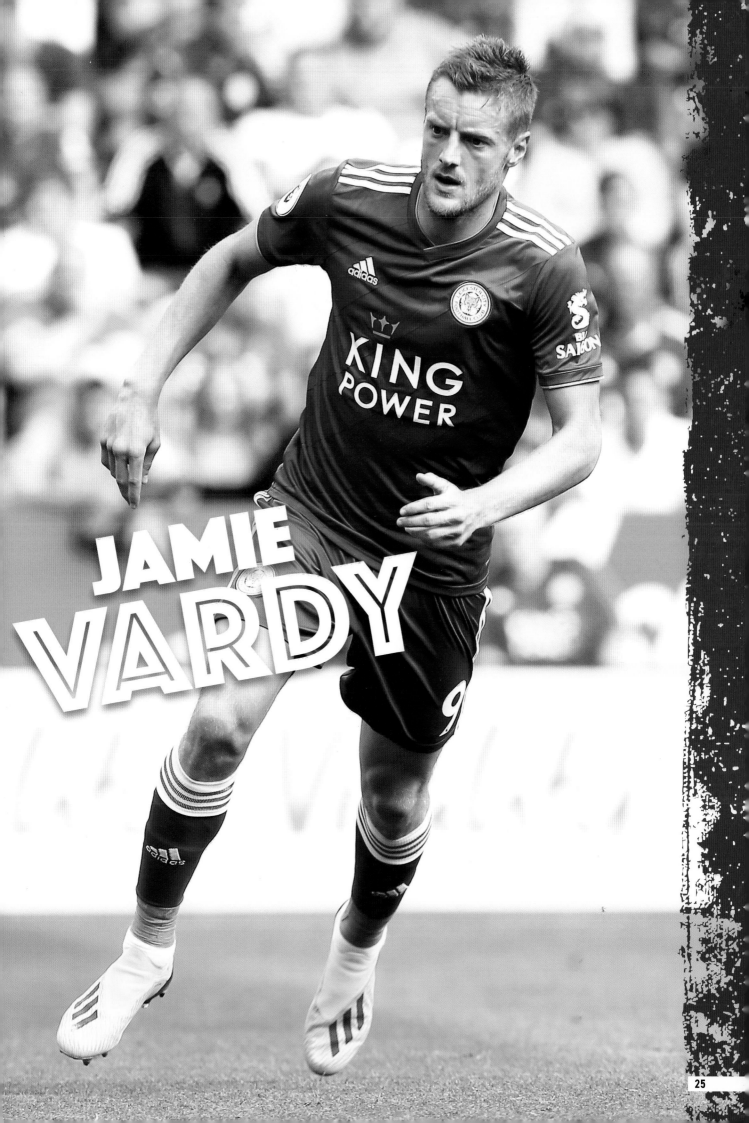

JAMIE
VARDY

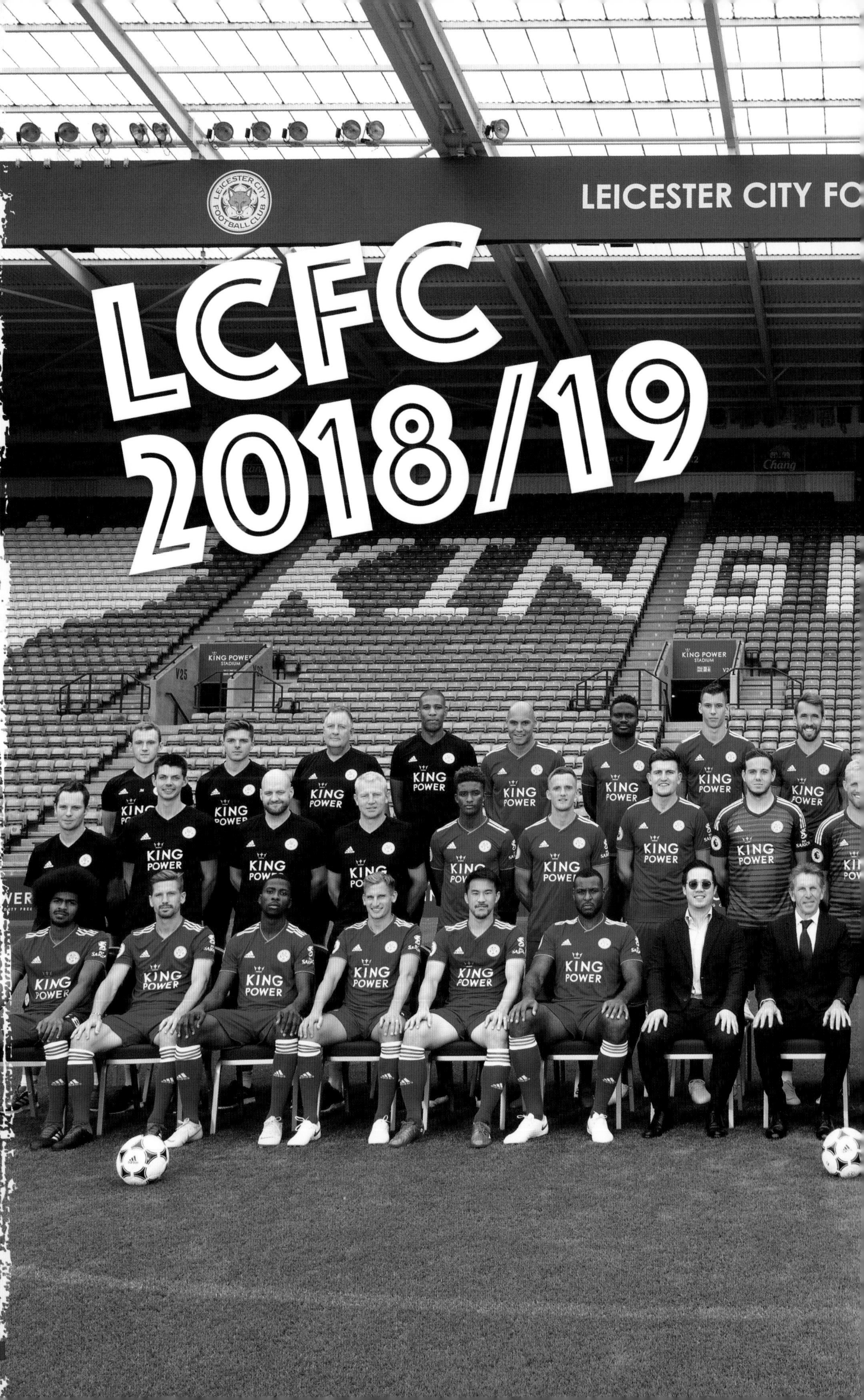

THE PUSKAS MOVE

Ferenc Puskas is one of the greatest footballers of all time and the creator of the famous 'V' move that you can see used in most games of football. It allows you to change direction quickly and fool your defender. The move is very simple but hard to master at speed.

TIP:
Use this move when you need to lose your defender. Pretend to strike the ball, your opponent will move to block your faked shot, allowing you to move freely in another direction.

TIP:
Always wait until your defender lunges for the ball before performing the Puskas move.

1. Start by dribbling the ball, keep it as near to your foot as possible while moving forward.

2. Move as if to kick the ball, but rather than striking it, bring your foot over the top of the ball.

TIP:
Don't perform this move too often or your opponents will learn to expect it!

3. Use the bottom of your foot to quickly drag the ball back to you.

4. Now change direction. You can finish the move with a shot at goal or by passing to a teammate.

JAMES MADDISON

BORN:

30 NOVEMBER 1960 · LEICESTER

POSITION:

STRIKER

FOXES DEBUT:

LEICESTER CITY 2-0 OLDHAM ATHLETIC · DIVISION TWO · 1 JANUARY 1979

ALL CLUBS:

LEICESTER CITY, EVERTON, BARCELONA, TOTTENHAM HOTSPUR, GRAMPUS EIGHT

FOXES APPEARANCES:

APPEARANCES	LEAGUE	FA CUP	LEAGUE CUP
216	194	13	9

FOXES GOALS:

GOALS	LEAGUE	FA CUP	LEAGUE CUP
103	95	6	2

STAT ATTACK
GARY LINEKER

ENGLAND INTERNATIONAL:

APPEARANCES	GOALS
80	48

INTERNATIONAL DEBUT:

26 MAY 1984 · SCOTLAND 1-1 ENGLAND

An extremely mobile striker with exceptional acceleration and a wonderful eye for goal, Gary Lineker soon began to make his mark at Filbert Street. Lineker became a regular name on the Foxes' teamsheet in 1981/82 and scored 19 goals in all competitions as Leicester enjoyed a memorable run to the FA Cup semi-final as a Second Division club.

The summer of 1982 saw Alan Smith arrive at Filbert Street, and he was paired with Lineker to devastating effect. The pair instantly hit it off with Lineker scoring 26 goals as the Foxes won promotion.

Lineker then enjoyed two remarkable seasons of top-flight football, a 22-goal haul in 1983/84 saw him second in the division's scoring charts and in 1984/85 he grabbed top slot with an impressive 24-goal return.

Sadly all good things come to an end, and after winning international recognition with England, Lineker had become a wanted man and joined League champions Everton in the summer of 1985 for a fee of £800,000.

A starring role in England's memorable 2018 World Cup campaign in Russia really was the icing on the cake of an incredible twelve months for Foxes' Player of the Season Harry Maguire.

Sheffield-born Maguire joined Leicester City in June 2017 from Hull City and the 25-year-old central defender went on to enjoy an outstanding debut season at the King Power Stadium.

His Foxes' debut came on the opening day of the season away to Arsenal and he then made a great impression on the home fans with a goal on his home debut as Leicester defeated Premier League new boys Brighton & Hove Albion 2-0. Maguire went on to be ever-present in the club's 2017/18 Premier League campaign. He netted a second goal for the club to secure a late point following a 2-2 draw with Manchester United at the King Power in December 2017. However, Maguire was brought to Leicester to prevent goals rather than score them and his defensive performances continued to be of the highest standard. Comfortable on the ball, strong in the tackle and an impressive ability to sense danger and deal with it – Maguire really has all the attributes that make the perfect defender.

He was unsurprisingly voted the Foxes' Player of the Season for 2016/17 and also the Players' Player of the Season.

With the Premier League campaign completed, Maguire then headed out to Russia as part of England's squad for the World Cup finals. His growing reputation then moved on another level following an excellent series of performances on the biggest stage of all. He picked the perfect moment to score his first international goal as he headed England in front in their quarter-final victory over Sweden.

Along with 'keeper Jordan Pickford and left-back Kieran Trippier, Maguire was one of the three surprise stars from an England side with reached the semi-final for the first time in 28 years.

PLAYER
OF THE SEASON

HARRY MAGUIRE

GOAL OF THE SEASON

Crowd favourite Jamie Vardy picked up Leicester City's Goal of the Season award for 2017/18 following his stunning goal in the Foxes' 4-1 win away to West Bromwich Albion in March 2018.

Claude Puel's team produced an impressive all-round display to come from behind to defeat the Baggies, but everyone was left talking about one goal in particular - Vardy's 21st minute equaliser.

Vardy's exquisite volley from Riyad Mahrez's inch-perfect pass from inside his own half was the standout moment in this away triumph. The goal won Vardy many plaudits, including Match of the Day pundit Frank Lampard, who described the goal as the best he had seen to-date in the 2017/18 campaign.

"This is my favourite goal of the season," said Lampard.

"The skill of his to run on to a straight ball and then end up putting it into the far corner, let's just look at his eyes because he can't see where the goal is because he has to focus on the ball.

"He is just going on instinct and adjusting every millisecond. He knows he can't put his foot through it because it is too difficult a skill so it is a controlled volley and he catches it absolutely perfect, and then, even better, he is right footed so that is his weaker foot.

"It certainly is a goal of the season contender and I absolutely love every aspect of that goal."

Even West Brom manager Alan Pardew said: "Even though it went against us and got them back in the game, you have to admit it was a great goal."

The goal spurred the Foxes on to a comfortable win as second-half goals from Riyad Mahrez, Kelechi Iheanacho and Vicente Iborra wrapped up the points.

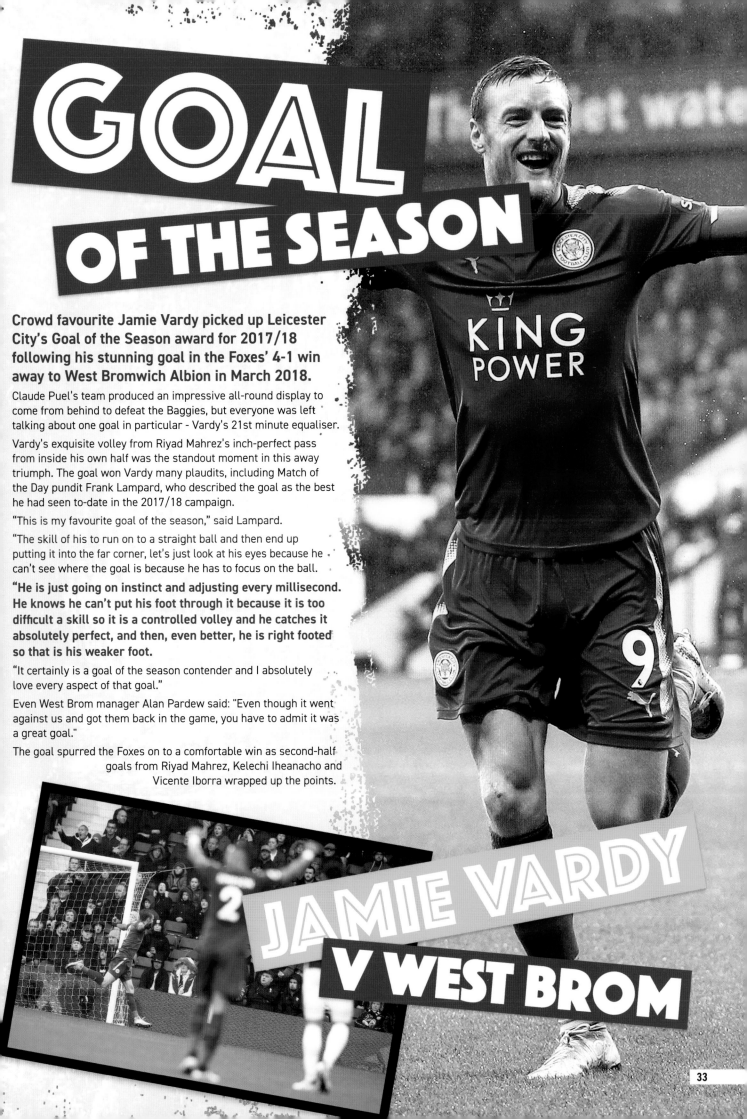

JAMIE VARDY V WEST BROM

GUESS THE CLUB

Can you work out which European club each set of clues is pointing to?

1 ANSWER

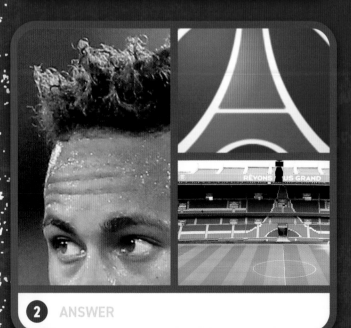

2 ANSWER

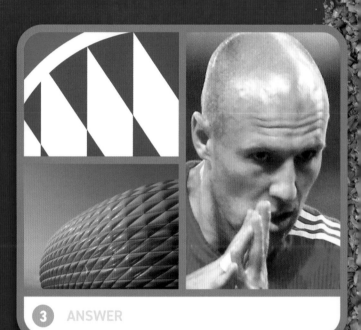

3 ANSWER

4 ANSWER

5 ANSWER

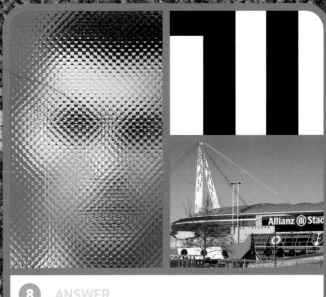

8 ANSWER

6 ANSWER

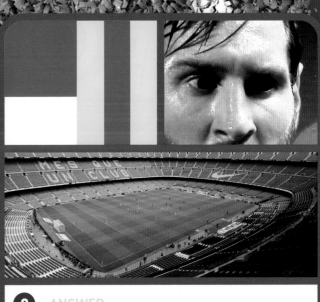

9 ANSWER

7 ANSWER

10 ANSWER

LOCAL HEROES

With Leicester City flying the flag for East Midlands football as the only club from the region in the Premier League, the Foxes are once again without a local derby in 2018/19 with the neighbouring clubs all currently playing at a lower level.

A majority of Foxes fans will point to Nottingham Forest and Derby County as the club's main rivals. An East Midlands derby match is any fixture involving two of the three clubs.

Leicester also has a rivalry with Coventry City, 24 miles away at the Ricoh Arena. The game between the two clubs has become known as the M69 derby, named after the M69 motorway that connects the two cities.

Here are three great derby day triumphs for the Foxes, one against each of our three main rivals.

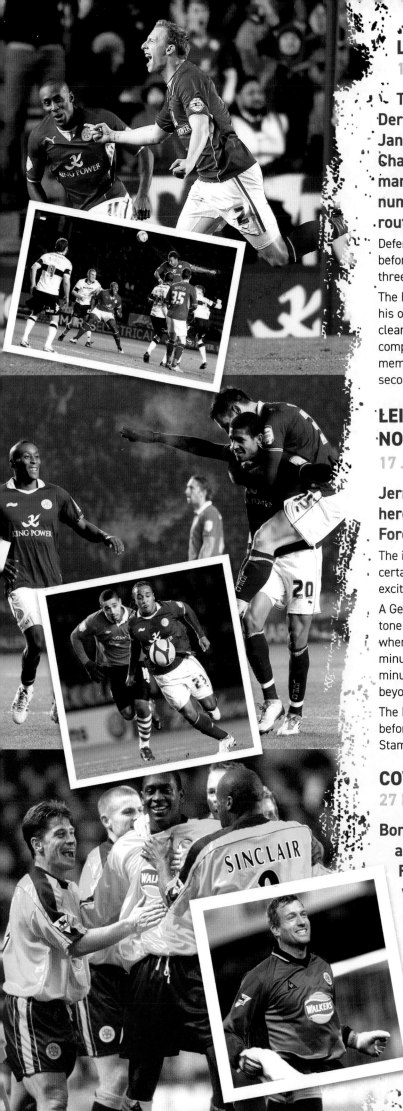

LEICESTER CITY 4 DERBY COUNTY 1
10 January 2014 · Championship

The Foxes thumped East Midlands rivals Derby County 4-1 at home on Friday 10 January 2014 during the club's 2013/14 Championship-winning season. Under the management of Nigel Pearson this was victory number five of a nine-match winning run en route to the Premier League.

Defender Ritchie de Laet opened the scoring after 25 minutes before leading scorer David Nugent doubled the Foxes' lead three minutes into the second half.

The Rams pulled a goal back when de Laet put the ball into his own net but within 60 seconds the hosts were two goals clear again as Nugent converted from the spot. Jamie Vardy completed the rout with the fourth goal, on what was a memorable evening for Leicester fans, midway through the second half.

LEICESTER CITY 4
NOTTINGHAM FOREST 0
17 January 2012 · FA Cup Third Round Replay

Jermaine Beckford was the Foxes' hat-trick hero as Leicester City brushed Nottingham Forest aside in this FA Cup third round replay.

The initial tie at the City Ground had ended 0-0 and the Foxes certainly made the most of home advantage to get an exciting FA Cup run underway.

A George Boateng own goal after just seven minutes set the tone for a difficult night for Forest, they then fell 2-0 down when Beckford registered his first goal of the night after 30 minutes. Beckford added further goals after 50 and 57 minutes to complete his treble and put the outcome well beyond doubt with half an hour still remaining.

The Foxes went on to defeat Swindon Town and Norwich City before bowing out to Chelsea in the quarter-final stage at Stamford Bridge.

COVENTRY CITY 0 LEICESTER CITY 1
27 November 1999 · Premier League

Born in Leicester, striker Emile Heskey knew all about the importance of local pride for Foxes' fans. Rather fitting therefore that it was he who netted the only goal of the game after an hour to give Leicester a top-flight double over the Sky Blues in 1999/2000.

Heskey's goal at Highfield Road gave the Leicester fans local bragging rights for the 1999/2000 campaign having also defeated Coventry earlier in the season at Filbert Street. A first-half penalty from Muzzy Izzet being the difference between the two sides on that occasion.

Magic MOMENT 118'

HESKEY TO THE *Rescue*

FIXTURE:	League Cup Final
DATE:	Sunday, 6 April 1997
SCORE:	Leicester City 1 Middlesbrough 1
VENUE:	Wembley
ATTENDANCE:	76,757

Emile Heskey struck a dramatic extra-time equaliser to ensure Martin O'Neill's side got a second bite of the cherry in their pursuit of League Cup glory.

O'Neill's men faced big-spending Middlesbrough in the 1997 League Cup final, where a hard-fought final saw very little between two evenly-matched sides. With the final goalless after 90 minutes the match headed into extra-time. It was soon first blood to Boro who opened the scoring after 95 minutes through Italian striker Fabrizio Ravanelli.

The Teeside club looked to be on the verge of their first piece of domestic cup silverware but two minutes from time Heskey rescued the Foxes and ensured the final would go to a replay.

A Steve Claridge goal in extra-time of the replay proved enough to win the cup for Leicester in the Hillsborough replay.

NAMPALYS MENDY

Can you identify all of these Foxes stars?

1

2

3

4

5

ANSWERS ON PAGE 62

WHO ARE YER?

6

7 POWER

8

9

10 G WER

DEMARAI
GRAY

#BOY'SGOTSKILLS

THE FLIP FLAP

Practise! Practise! Practise!

1. Start by getting familiar with the leg movement.

Push the ball with the outside of your foot.

TIP: Try performing the movement while hopping

TIP: Practise performing the movement while moving forwards and backwards

2. Then move your foot around the ball and bring it back in towards your body.

AKA 'the Elastico'

This move is used by many players and was made famous first by Rivelino in the 1970s and more recently by Ronaldinho. It is a simple technique and done right, really works! The idea behind it is to unbalance your defender by moving the ball one way before using some tricky footwork to move off in another direction!

3. Once you're familiar with the movement, try it while dribbling the ball forward.

TIP: Work on perfecting the technique, then when you're ready you can start moving the ball further away from your body to really confuse your defender

4. Push the ball with the outside of your foot, away from your body. As your defender moves in the direction of the ball...

5. ...Move your foot around the ball, drag it back across your body and move off in the other direction.

43

≪ REWIND

We take a look at three great Foxes games from last season...

LEICESTER CITY 3 HUDDERSFIELD TOWN 0
PREMIER LEAGUE · 1 JANUARY 2018

The Foxes began the New Year with a 3-0 thumping of Premier League new boys Huddersfield Town at the King Power Stadium.

Although the Terriers proved to be something of a surprise package in 2017/18 and maintained their Premier League status, they had no answer to a blistering second-half performance from a Leicester side that got the calendar year of 2018 off to the best possible start.

Riyad Mahrez opened the scoring after 53 minutes, with Islam Silmani doubling the home side's lead on the hour mark. Marc Albrighton completed the rout in the last minute to send the Foxes' fans home happy.

WEST BROM 1 LEICESTER CITY 4
PREMIER LEAGUE · 10 MARCH 2018

Leicester City heaped the pressure on beleaguered West Brom boss Alan Pardew, with a 4-1 victory over the relegation-haunted Baggies in March 2018.

The hosts had taken the lead through Salomon Rondon, but Leicester equalised in spectacular fashion when Jamie Vardy volleyed crisply past Ben Foster from Riyad Mahrez's ball over the top.

After the break Mahrez then got on the scoresheet himself when he coolly finished after a clever pass from Kelechi Iheanacho.

Former Manchester City striker Iheanacho put the game beyond Albion when he headed in Ben Chilwell's cross. Leicester completed the rout in injury time when Vicente Iborra headed home from a corner.

LEICESTER CITY 3 ARSENAL 1
PREMIER LEAGUE · 9 MAY 2018

Claude Puel's men ended their programme of 2017/18 home fixtures with a resounding 3-1 victory over Arsenal.

The win earned the Foxes a first Premier League triumph over Arsenal since 1994 as Arsene Wenger's penultimate game in charge of the Gunners ended in defeat.

Kelechi Iheanacho rifled the opener past Petr Cech after poor defending from the visitors, who had 20-year-old defender Konstantinos Mavropanos sent off 92 seconds later for hauling down Iheanacho as he broke through on goal.

Arsenal levelled through Pierre-Emerick Aubameyang, but Jamie Vardy's penalty, awarded after Henrikh Mkhitaryan brought down Demarai Gray, and Riyad Mahrez's late breakaway goal sealed victory for the Foxes.

1 How many points did the Foxes finish last season with?

ANSWER

2 Who was the last player to join the Foxes on a permanent deal in the January 2018 transfer window?

ANSWER

3 Who top scored last season with 20 league goals?

ANSWER

4 Which team did the Foxes knock out in the fifth round of the FA Cup?

ANSWER

5 How many clean sheets did the Foxes keep in the Premier League in 2017/18?

ANSWER

6 Who made the most Premier League appearances in 2017/18?

ANSWER

2017/18 END OF TERM EXAM

How much did you learn about the Foxes' last campaign?

7 Who was City's first win of the 2017/18 season against?

ANSWER

8 Which Foxes player received the most yellow cards in the Premier League last season?

ANSWER

9 Who put in the most tackles, with 138, last season?

ANSWER

10 How many goals did Leicester City score in the Premier League last season?

ANSWER

ANSWERS ON PAGE 62

We take a look at three important matches coming up for the Foxes in the second half of the season...

FAST FORWARD »

LEICESTER CITY V MAN UNITED
PREMIER LEAGUE · 2 FEBRUARY 2019

The Foxes will face Manchester United in their first Premier League fixture of February. The match is in the middle of three mouth-watering clashes that see Leicester play Liverpool away, the Red Devils at home and then head off to face Tottenham Hotspur.

Last season's meeting with United at the King Power Stadium proved to be a thrilling affair as a last-gasp Harry Maguire goal ensured a 2-2 draw, and a share of the spoils for a Leicester team that had opened the scoring through Jamie Vardy.

As always the United squad will be packed with international superstars and the fixture remains one of the highlights of the Foxes' calendar.

TOTTENHAM HOTSPUR V LEICESTER CITY
PREMIER LEAGUE · 9 FEBRUARY 2019

Saturday, 9 February 2019 is sure to be a date noted in many Foxes' fan's diaries with Leicester City due to make their first ever trip to Tottenham Hotspur's new ground.

A Leicester City fixture on a new ground is always an exciting occasion, and after so many memorable visits to White Hart Lane down the years, it will be intriguing to see the new stadium that has been constructed on the old site, while Spurs have been away at Wembley.

Last season Leicester defeated Spurs 2-1 at the King Power Stadium, before a nine-goal thriller ended in Spurs favour (5-4) as the 2017/18 campaign came to a close at Wembley.

LEICESTER CITY V CHELSEA
PREMIER LEAGUE · 12 MAY 2019

Leicester City wrap up their 2018/19 campaign with a high-profile match at home to 2016/17 Premier League champions Chelsea.

Former Foxes star and 2018 World Cup winner N'Golo Kante struck the winning goal for Chelsea as the Blues secured a 2-1 triumph on their last visit to the King Power in September 2017.

The Stamford Bridge club are now under the management of Italian boss Maurizio Sarri and have both Kante and another former title-winning Fox in Danny Drinkwater in their squad.

Despite the wait to the end of the season, this is sure to be a King Power clash well worth waiting for.

PREDICTION FOR 3RD AND 4TH PLACE CHAMPIONS LEAGUE QUALIFICATION:

Manchester Utd & Arsenal

YOUR PREDICTION:

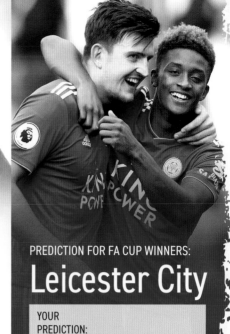

PREDICTION FOR FA CUP WINNERS:

Leicester City

YOUR PREDICTION:

PREDICTION FOR PREMIER LEAGUE WINNERS:

Liverpool

YOUR PREDICTION:

PREDICTION FOR PREMIER LEAGUE RUNNERS-UP:

Manchester City

YOUR PREDICTION:

PREDICTION FOR PREMIER LEAGUE RELEGATION:

Newcastle Utd, Huddersfield Town & Southampton

YOUR PREDICTION:

2018/19 PREDICTIONS

Here are our predictions for the 2018/19 season.

What do you think will happen?

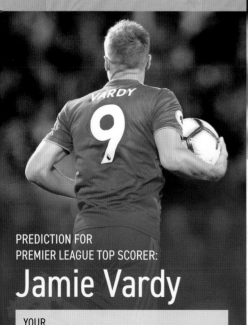

PREDICTION FOR PREMIER LEAGUE TOP SCORER:

Jamie Vardy

YOUR PREDICTION:

PREDICTION FOR PREMIER LEAGUE PLAYER OF THE SEASON:

Kevin De Bruyne

YOUR PREDICTION:

PREDICTION FOR LEAGUE CUP WINNERS:

Burnley

YOUR PREDICTION:

#BOY'S GOT SKILLS
THE OKOCHA STEP OVER

Jay-Jay Okocha was one of the best tricksters the Premier League has ever seen. He was effortless in getting past his opponents and here we take a look at how to perform one of his most famous moves...

1. While running...
...roll the ball with the inside of your right foot across your body to the left.

2. Fake like you're going to hit it with your left foot...

TIP:
Roll the ball far enough out across your body so it doesn't get stuck under your feet.

Tip:
Practise until you can master the move off both feet!

3. ...but step over it instead!

4. While you're performing the step over...
...do a quick body feint to the right to help throw off your opponent.

5. Continue going left...

...leaving your opponent wondering what just happened!

HARRY
MAGUIRE

GREAT GAFFERS

The Foxes have been blessed with a host of great managers over the years - here we take a brief look at four of our finest.

MARTIN O'NEILL

After joining the Foxes from Norwich City in December 1995, Martin O'Neill overcame a difficult first few months in the Filbert Street hot-seat before guiding the team to the end-of-season play-offs. The Foxes sneaked into the play-offs with a sixth placed finish and won promotion after defeating Crystal Palace in the Wembley final.

Back in the Premier League and O'Neill made several shrewd signings as the club established itself among the big boys with ninth, tenth and eighth placed finishes under O'Neill's watch. The club also enjoyed two League Cup triumphs, firstly in 1997 and again in 2000. Those League Cup victories resulted in qualification for the UEFA Cup in 1997/98 and again in 2000/01.

Certainly one of the club's finest managers, O'Neill has since managed at Celtic, Aston Villa and Sunderland plus internationally with the Republic of Ireland.

MICKY ADAMS

Following a successful period as manager of Fulham, Micky Adams took in brief spells at Fulham and Nottingham Forest before becoming Brighton & Hove Albion boss in April 1999.

He led the Seagulls to the Third Division title in 2000/01 and then stepped up to the Premier League when he joined Leicester City in October 2001 as assistant to then Foxes' boss Dave Bassett.

After the club were relegated in 2002, Bassett became Director of Football and Adams took charge of first team affairs. His first season in charge proved to be a great success as he guided the club back to the Premier League at the first time of asking. The Foxes amassed an impressive 92 points and ended the season as Championship runners-up, six points behind champions Portsmouth and twelve points ahead of third placed Sheffield United.

NIGEL PEARSON

Nigel Pearson enjoyed two successful spells as Foxes' manager. Pearson's first reign at Leicester began in June 2008 when he was charged with attempting to get the club out of the third tier of English football, following relegation the previous season.

He made an excellent start to life at the Walkers Stadium, winning three of his first four games and was named August Manager of the Month in League One. The impressive start set the tone for the season as Leicester won the League One title with a 96-point tally.

Pearson's second spell began in November 2011 with the Leicester sitting in the middle of the Championship. After guiding the team to the play-off semi-finals the following season, Pearson went one better in 2013/14 as the Foxes won the title and promotion to the Premier League. In 2014/15 he inspired the team to top-flight survival while laying the foundations for the success that followed in 2015/16.

CLAUDIO RANIERI

A vastly experienced manager, Claudio Ranieri took charge of Leicester City in July 2015 as successor to Nigel Pearson who had overseen the Foxes' great escape just two months earlier.

The Italian arrived with an impressive CV having managed some of Europe's top clubs. He also had knowledge of the English Premier League having spent a lengthy period in charge at Chelsea.

Ranieri had gained a 'tinker man' reputation for his constant team changes and his appointment at Leicester was met with scepticism in some quarters.

However, the Foxes defeated Sunderland 4-2 at home in their opening game of the season and triggered the beginning of the most amazing season in the club's history. Against all odds, Ranieri guided the unfancied Foxes to the 2015/16 Premier League title.

FIRST ELEVEN

Choose your all-time First Eleven, put their names and numbers on the back of the shirts, then colour them in!

SPOT THE BALL

The ball is missing from this photo, where should it be?

WHAT BALL?

Can you figure out which is the real ball in this photo?

ANSWERS ON PAGE 62

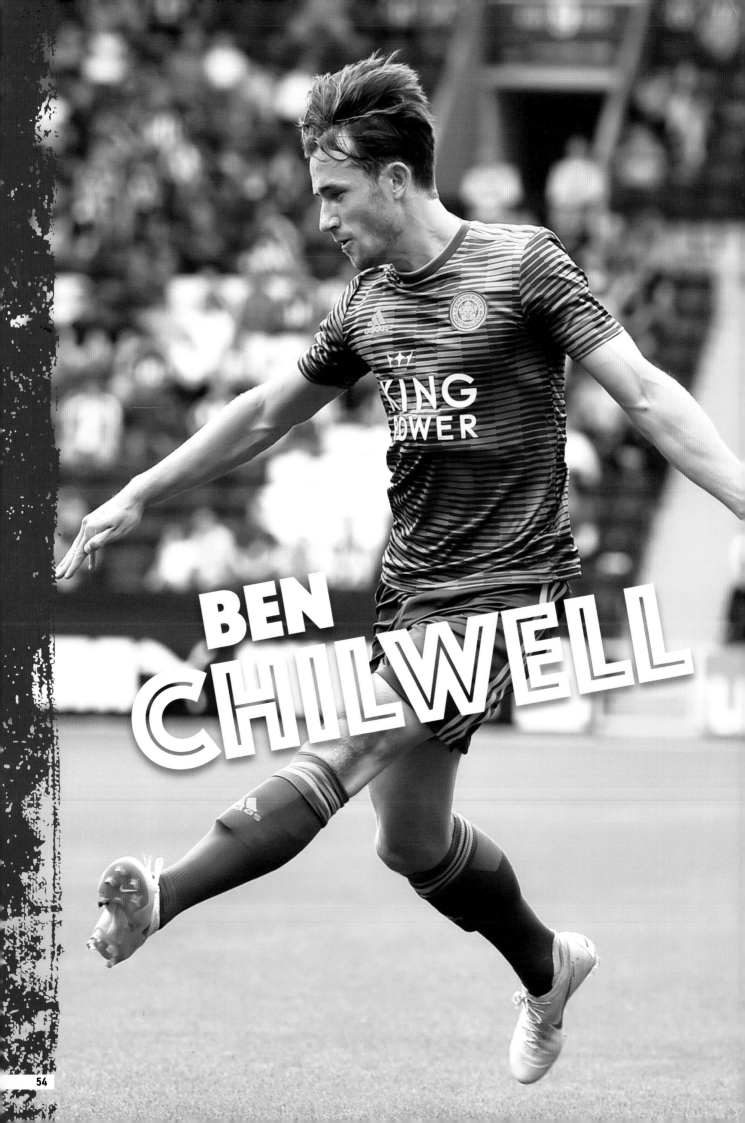

BEN
CHILWELL

BORN:

3 NOVEMBER 1964 · PRESTON

POSITION:

CENTRAL DEFENDER

FOXES DEBUT:

LEICESTER CITY 1-1 LUTON TOWN
DIVISION ONE · 23 SEPTEMBER 1986

ALL CLUBS:

WIGAN ATHLETIC, LEICESTER CITY, NORWICH CITY, COVENTRY CITY

FOXES PLAYER OF THE SEASON:

1987-88

FOXES APPEARANCES:

APPEARANCES	LEAGUE	FA CUP	LEAGUE CUP	OTHERS
451	369	17	40	25

FOXES GOALS:

GOALS	LEAGUE	FA CUP	LEAGUE CUP	OTHERS
62	53	1	4	4

STAT ATTACK
STEVE WALSH

Defender Steve Walsh joined the Foxes from Wigan Athletic for a fee of £100,000 in 1986 and went on to play over 450 games for the club and etch his name into Leicester City folklore.

Under the management of Brian Little, Walsh was named Leicester City captain. A clear leader and organiser of the defence, his talents were also employed in a more advanced role under Little, and he scored 15 league goals in the 1992/93 season as the club reached the First Division Play-Off final.

Walsh celebrated arguably his finest hour with the club during the 1994 First Division Play-Off final at Wembley when his two goals ensured a memorable 2-1 victory over Derby County.

Under Martin O'Neill, Walsh was part of the Foxes' team that won promotion via the play-offs in 1996 and tasted League Cup glory in 1997.

HERO HUNT

Here is a list of 20 Foxes heroes. All but one of their surnames are hidden in the grid...

...can you work out who is missing?

```
E T M O R G A N E Q G Y C J R O L G F E B M
D X F B C R E D N H Z A D C H R N B H K G G
H J A J G E D Y I T P R F R N D I Y F W I F
K F U L B B A S C R A O U I A X K M J H C A
Z A L B A O B S O P W G V R E V O L G I E N
Y U N Q H J D E T E B S E F X Z Y U K T E H
S C K M X S M O I P A U H Y L E Q O C W L C
C F E R O I R G N X D J D T K W F A P O I I
I R U H T E T I S K W U A S D B T O Q R Z B
P G Z Z L J W L I N E K E R M J A J I T O P
E W J L Q V P E K W L H Y K O Y D S C H B W
U S E O R P L N A M S Q L O C B G E X I W H
Y W I T D V M N A A O Z E P D M E B C D N U
W O K A L P H O M N T B Y P L N M R T R V Z
M R M W I B A N K S A V E R U C J I T G F S
C T B E X S R E O A P N L J Z H S X R S U G
G H L J A N K J W V B T W E J A S D H I M V
N I A S Q F O L R A J M O B A N L I Q K Y W
Y N R N O B H L X G N D R Y F O L Q N E U H
U G A K D F I A Z E S O J A L T F O B C U I
O T W O E L K M U C V G I S O K O T A P H X
T O Q C K J E E N P G K E N D I Z Z E T H Y
L N P F D T G R V Y K C H R M F P S N T A H
N Y X H T W S U R T T O I L L E T F E S W Y
U Z J I Z P R M I D Q L G O W R A T U B G S
```

Gordon **Banks**	Muzzy **Izzet**	Iwan **Roberts**	Jamie **Vardy**
Arthur **Chandler**	Neil **Lennon**	Arthur **Rowley**	Steve **Walsh**
Matt **Elliott**	Gary **Lineker**	Robbie **Savage**	Keith **Weller**
Len **Glover**	Wes **Morgan**	Peter **Shilton**	Steve **Whitworth**
Emile **Heskey**	David **Nish**	John **Sjoberg**	Frank **Worthington**

RLVOELPOI
1

ALUMHF
2

FEEHFLDIS NIEUDT
3

RNGBIHMMIA TIYC
4

TEWS AMH DUTNIE
5

YCTSLRA LAPEAC
6

Here are the away shirts of twelve Premier League and Championship clubs, but their team names have been jumbled up!

Can you figure out who's who?

SHIRT SHUFFLE

OONEUMTBRUH
7

NQESEU RKAP GRARNES
8

KOETS TCIY
9

WESATNELC TUNEDI
10

ROTPENS HRTNO NDE
11

NATOS LAVIL
12

Magic MOMENT

17'

FOXES WITHIN TOUCHING *Distance*

FIXTURE:	Barclays Premier League
DATE:	Sunday, 1 May 2016
SCORE:	Manchester United 1 Leicester City 1
VENUE:	Old Trafford
ATTENDANCE:	75,275

Captain Wes Morgan headed home the goal that moved the Foxes to within two points of the Premier League title.

After falling behind to an Anthony Martial goal after just eight minutes at Old Trafford, Morgan headed home nine minutes later to earn the Foxes a point from this tense and tricky trip to Manchester.

In what was a fairytale season for the club, Morgan's goal ensured that just two more points would see Claudio Ranieri's men crowned the most unlikely of Premier League champions.

In the end no more points were needed, as Tottenham Hotspur suffered a defeat to Chelsea the next day and Leicester City were 2015/16 Premier League Champions!

RICARDO

How's your knowledge of the laws of the game?
You think you can do better than the man in the middle?
here's your chance to prove it...

HEY REF!

1. Jamie Vardy shoots for goal from 25 yards. His fierce drive deflects off your head, wrong-footing the keeper, on its way into the back of the net. What's your call?

A: You award an indirect free-kick to the opposition.
B: It's a goal!
C: You give a drop-ball from where you were hit with ball.

2. James Maddison strikes for goal from six yards, but as he shoots, the ball bursts and stops just before the goal line. Alert, he follows up and taps the ball home. What's your call?

A: It's a goal!
B: You award a penalty kick to the Foxes.
C: No goal and you restart with a drop ball where the ball burst.

3. James Maddison sends the keeper the wrong way from the penalty spot, but his effort hits the post and rebounds straight to Jamie Vardy who rifles the ball into the net to score. What is your decision?

A: It's a goal!
B: The spot kick has to be retaken.
C: You award an indirect free-kick to the opposition.

VARDY

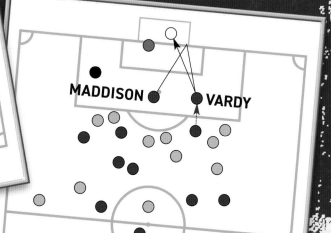

MADDISON   VARDY

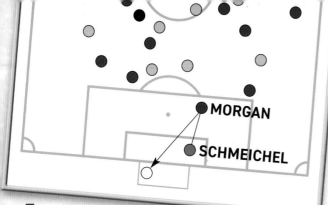

MORGAN

SCHMEICHEL

4. Kasper Schmeichel attempts to take a quick goal kick, but to his horror, it hits Wes Morgan who is still in the penalty area and the ball deflects into his own net. What's your call, ref?

A: It's a goal!

B: A corner kick to the opposing team

C: The goal kick has to be retaken.

5. Standing in his own penalty area, Kasper Schmeichel catches the ball directly from teammate Wes Morgan's throw-in. What is your decision?

A: Everything's fine. Play on.

B: You award the opposing team an indirect free-kick.

C: A yellow card for Schmeichel and a penalty for the opposing team.

SCHMEICHEL

MORGAN

6. You have decided Jamie Vardy's spot kick must be re-taken after an infringement by the keeper. This time Shinji Okazaki steps forward to take the kick. Is that allowed?

A: No, I award an indirect free kick to the opposition.

B: Yes, any Foxes player can re-take the penalty.

C: No, the player who took the initial spot kick, Jamie Vardy, must retake the kick.

7. You have awarded a drop ball. As you drop the ball, Wes Morgan and the opposing player both kick the ball at exactly the same time before it hits the turf. What's your ruling?

A: You show a yellow card to both players for ungentlemanly conduct.

B: You drop the ball again.

C: Play on.

MADDISON

8. James Maddison is on the scoresheet again, tapping in from only three yards out. When he scores, he is slightly ahead of the last defender, but in line with the goalkeeper. What is your decision?

A: Goal. In line with the keeper is not offside.

B: Goal disallowed. Maddison is offside. To be onside, he must be in line with the second last opponent or the ball.

C: Goal. A player can't be offside inside the six-yard box.

9. Jamie Vardy takes a long throw in aiming for the head of Ben Chilwell. No-one makes contact with the ball and it bounces into the net direct from Vardy's throw. What's your call, ref?

A: Goal. Providing there was an attempt to play the ball.

B: Goal. As long as the throw-in was taken correctly.

C: No Goal. A goal can never be scored direct from a throw in.

ANSWERS ON PAGE 62

ANSWERS

PAGE 22 · SPOT THE DIFFERENCE

PAGE 34 · GUESS THE CLUB

1. Ajax. 2. Paris Saint-Germain. 3. Bayern Munich. 4. Sporting Lisbon.
5. Real Madrid. 6. Arsenal. 7. Celtic. 8. Juventus. 9. Barcelona. 10. Club Brugge.

PAGE 40 · WHO ARE YER?

1. Wilfred Ndidi. 2. Vicente Iborra. 3. Fousseni Diabate. 4. Harry Maguire.
5. Christian Fuchs. 6. Marc Albrighton. 7. Wes Morgan. 8. James Maddison.
9. Hamzah Choudhury. 10. Danny Simpson.

PAGE 45 · 2017/18 END OF TERM EXAM

1. 47. 2. Fousseni Diabaté. 3. Jamie Vardy. 4. Sheffield United.
5. Nine. 6. Harry Maguire, 38 appearances. 7. Brighton & Hove Albion.
8. Harry Maguire, 7 yellow cards. 9. Onyinye Wilfred Ndidi. 10. 56.

PAGE 53 · SPOT THE BALL

PAGE 53 · WHAT BALL?

Ball F.

PAGE 56 · HERO HUNT

Steve Walsh.

PAGE 57 · SHIRT SHUFFLE

1. Liverpool. 2. Fulham. 3. Sheffield United. 4. Birmingham City.
5. West Ham United. 6. Crystal Palace. 7. Bournemouth. 8. Queens Park Rangers.
9. Stoke City. 10. Newcastle United. 11. Preston North End. 12. Aston Villa.

PAGE 60 · HEY REF!

1. B. 2. C. 3. A. 4. C. 5. B. 6. B. 7. B. 8. B. 9. C.